SUCCESSFUL ENTREPRENEUR MINDSET

Unlock the Power of Your Mind
to Achieve Success

Ray Goodwin

CONTENTS

LIABILITY DISCLAIMER

The information contained within this book is intended for informational purposes only and should not be construed as legal or professional advice. The authors and publishers of this book are not responsible for any losses or damages that may arise from the use of the information contained within.

The reader assumes full responsibility for any decisions made based on the information in this book. The authors and publishers do not endorse any particular method, service or product mentioned in this book and are not responsible for any consequences resulting from their use.

The reader should exercise caution and discretion when making life changing decisions, and should be aware of the risks and potential consequences of their actions. This book is not a substitute for professional or legal advice and should not be relied upon as such.

By reading and using the information in this book, the reader acknowledges and agrees to hold harmless the authors, publishers, and any other parties involved in the creation or distribution of this book from any and all liability, claims, damages, or losses that may arise from their use of the information contained herein.

CHAPTER 1: UNDERSTANDING THE ENTREPRENEURIAL MINDSET

Being an entrepreneur is not an easy task. It requires a specific mindset that helps you navigate the ups and downs of business ownership. As someone who has been in the online sales game since it began, I have seen many aspiring entrepreneurs fail. But I have also seen many succeed beyond their wildest dreams.

What separates successful entrepreneurs from those who never quite make it? The answer lies in their mindset. This is what prompted me to write this book – to share with you the secrets of the successful entrepreneur mindset.

The journey towards becoming a successful entrepreneur starts with developing certain qualities and habits that create a strong foundation for success. These include things like resilience, self-discipline, and passion. However, there are also key strategies that successful entrepreneurs employ to stay ahead of the curve and overcome obstacles.

In Successful Entrepreneur Mindset, you'll learn how to cultivate these essential qualities and strategies through real-life examples and actionable advice. This book will help you shift your mindset so you can confidently take on challenges, embrace uncertainty, and achieve your goals as an entrepreneur. So join me on this journey towards success and let's build your entrepreneurial mindset together!

Overview

Have you ever had a business idea that you couldn't shake off? Do you find yourself constantly thinking of new ways to solve problems in your community or industry? If so, you may have an entrepreneurial mindset. This mindset is characterized by a unique set of skills, attitudes, and behaviors that enable individuals to identify opportunities, take risks, and create something out of nothing.

But what exactly is an entrepreneur? An entrepreneur is someone who starts a business or creates a product or service with the aim of making a profit. However, entrepreneurship is not just about making money. It's about creating value for others, solving problems, and making a difference in the world.

So what are the characteristics of a successful entrepreneur? A successful entrepreneur is someone who is passionate, innovative, resilient, and adaptable. They are not afraid to take risks, and they use failure as a learning opportunity. They are constantly seeking new opportunities for growth and development, and they have the ability to think creatively and outside the box.

One of the most important aspects of being an entrepreneur is having an entrepreneurial mindset. This mindset is characterized by the ability to think strategically, take calculated risks, and learn from failure. It involves having a growth mindset, where failures are seen as opportunities for growth and learning. This mindset also involves having a desire to continually learn and improve, as well as a willingness to take action and pursue opportunities.

So how does having an entrepreneurial mindset differ from having an employee mindset? An employee mindset is focused on job security, stability, and following rules and procedures. Employees typically have a fixed mindset, where they believe their skills and abilities are predetermined and cannot be changed. On the other hand, entrepreneurs have a growth mindset, where they believe they can constantly improve and learn new skills. They are also focused on taking risks and creating opportunities for themselves.

So how can you cultivate an entrepreneurial mindset? The first step is to start thinking like an entrepreneur. This means focusing on opportunities, thinking creatively, and being open to new ideas. You should also embrace failure and see it as a learning opportunity rather than a setback. Developing a growth mindset and a willingness to take action are also key components of an entrepreneurial mindset.

But why is having an entrepreneurial mindset so important? The benefits of having this mindset go beyond just starting a business. An entrepreneurial mindset can help you become more successful in your career, improve your problem-solving skills, and even improve your personal relationships. It can also help you develop a greater sense of purpose and fulfillment in your life.

There are also many common myths about entrepreneurship that need to be debunked. For example, some people believe that entrepreneurs are born, not made. However, research has shown that anyone can develop an entrepreneurial mindset with the right mindset and training. Another myth is that entrepreneurs are always successful. In reality, failure is a common experience for entrepreneurs, and it's often necessary for learning and growth.

This book will provide you with the knowledge and skills you need to develop a successful entrepreneurial mindset. From identifying your passion to building a professional network, to developing a marketing strategy and overcoming fear and failure, this book covers everything you need to know to become a successful entrepreneur. So let's get started on this exciting journey of entrepreneurship together.

CHAPTER 2:
IDENTIFYING
YOUR PASSION

The journey of entrepreneurship can be a challenging one, but it will all be worth it if you are doing something you are passionate about. Passion is the driving force that keeps you motivated to overcome obstacles and take your business from an idea to a reality. In this chapter, we will explore the importance of identifying your passion and aligning it with your business idea.

Why passion is important for entrepreneurship

Passion is essential for entrepreneurs because it is the fuel that keeps you going. Starting a business is not easy, and there will be times when you encounter challenges that will make you want to quit. However, if you're passionate about your idea, you will keep pushing forward until you succeed. A business born out of passion will motivate you, energize you, and give you a purpose. You will work tirelessly to make it successful, and you will be proud of what you've accomplished.

Methods for discovering your passion

Discovering your passion can be a daunting task, but it doesn't have to be. The first step is to think about your hobbies and interests. What do you enjoy doing in your spare time? What are you truly passionate about?

Another method is to think about the things that frustrate you or the problems that you would like to solve. Often, the best businesses arise from identifying a problem and finding a solution. For example, if you're frustrated with the lack of eco-friendly cleaning products in the market and are passionate about the environment, starting a company that produces green cleaning products could be an excellent idea.

You can also ask yourself what you would do if money wasn't an issue. If you had all the money in the world, what would you do with your time? What would give you the most satisfaction and fulfillment?

Importance of aligning your passion with your business idea

Once you have identified your passion, the next step is to align it with your business idea. The best way to do this is to choose an industry or niche that excites you. When you're passionate about what you're doing, it will show in everything you do. You will be a more motivated, driven, and creative entrepreneur.

It's also essential to ensure that your business idea aligns with your core values. For example, if you're passionate about environmental sustainability, starting a business that disregards eco-friendliness would be a contradiction.

Examples of successful entrepreneurs who followed their passion

There are countless examples of entrepreneurs who have built thriving businesses based on their passion. One such person is Elon Musk, who is passionate about science and technology. He started SpaceX to accomplish his goal of colonizing Mars, and Tesla to revolutionize the automobile industry with sustainable energy.

Another example is Oprah Winfrey, who is passionate about media and self-improvement. She turned her passion into a media empire, and her talk show, The Oprah Winfrey Show, became a platform for helping people improve their lives.

Overcoming obstacles to pursuing your passion

The road to pursuing your passion is not always easy. There will be obstacles that you will face along the way. It's essential to prepare yourself mentally and emotionally to overcome them.

One of the most common obstacles is fear. Fear of failure, fear of the unknown, fear of not being good enough, and fear of what others will think. To overcome your fears, you need to acknowledge them, understand where they come from, and take action regardless.

Another obstacle is self-doubt. You may doubt your ability to succeed or think that you don't have what it takes. To overcome self-doubt, you need to remember why you started in the first place and focus on your strengths.

Importance of regularly evaluating and reassessing your passion

Once you have identified your passion and aligned it with your business idea, it's essential to regularly evaluate and reassess it. As you gain more experience, your passions may change, and your business may need to evolve along with it. Set aside time periodically to reflect on your passion and see if it's still aligned with your business goals.

How to incorporate your passion into your business strategy

To incorporate your passion into your business strategy, you need to:

❖ Know your passion: identify what you're passionate about and what makes you tick.

❖ Understand the market: research the market and identify gaps or opportunities where you can apply your passion.

❖ Develop a plan: create a strategy that incorporates your passion and aligns with your goals.

❖ Communicate with stakeholders: share your passion with employees, investors, and customers, and use it to differentiate your business from competitors.

Developing a mission statement based on your passion

A mission statement is a powerful tool that communicates your passion, values, and purpose to stakeholders. Your mission statement should be concise, meaningful, and focused on your passion and the value your business provides. A well-crafted mission statement can serve as the foundation of your business and guide you in making critical decisions.

In conclusion, identifying and aligning your passion with your business idea is a crucial step in becoming a successful entrepreneur. It's the driving force that will motivate you to overcome challenges and lead you to success. Take the time to discover your passion, and continue to evaluate and align it with your business strategy. With passion and persistence, you can achieve anything you set your mind to.

CHAPTER 3: DEVELOPING A BUSINESS PLAN

When starting a new business venture, it is essential to have a solid plan in place. A business plan serves as a road map for your company's success, outlining the steps necessary to achieve your goals. In this chapter, we will discuss the purpose of a business plan, the key components it should include, and tips for writing a successful one.

Purpose of a Business Plan

A business plan is a written document outlining your company's goals and strategies for achieving them. Its purpose is to provide clarity and direction while also serving as a tool for attracting investors and securing funding. A well-written business plan will articulate your company's vision, mission, strategic objectives, market analysis, marketing plan, financial projections, and risks, among other factors.

Key Components of a Business Plan

A business plan should consist of the following key components:

❖ Executive Summary: A brief summary of your company's vision, mission, and goals.

❖ Company Description: A detailed description of your company, including its history, products, and services.

❖ Market Analysis: An analysis of your market, including information about your target audience, competitors, and industry trends.

❖ Marketing Plan: A description of your marketing strategy, including pricing, promotion, and distribution.

❖ Financial Planning and Budgeting: A detailed financial forecast outlining your company's revenue projections, cash flow, and expenses.

❖ Goals and Measuring Progress: A clear definition of your company's objectives and how progress will be measured.

Tips for Writing a Successful Business Plan

Now that we have covered the essential elements of a business plan let's discuss some tips for writing a successful one:

❖ Research and Conduct Market Analysis: It is crucial to conduct proper market research to ensure that your business idea is viable. Analyze the current market trends, assess the demand for your product or service, and identify your target audience. This will help you to tailor your product or service to your audience and ensure that you have a profitable business model.

❖ Define Your Target Audience: Knowing who your target audience is will help you to focus your marketing efforts. When writing your business plan, describe your target audience in detail and outline how you plan to reach them.

❖ Create a Marketing Strategy: A solid marketing strategy is essential for your company's success. Outline your pricing strategy, branding, advertising, and sales methods. Consider avenues like social media, press releases, influencer marketing, and other powerful marketing tools.

❖ Focus on Your Financials: Your financial projections will be one of the most critical elements of your business plan. Be sure to provide a detailed forecast of your revenue and expenses for several years. Outline your funding requirements, including how much money you need and where you plan to obtain it.

❖ Set Goals and Define Metrics for Success: Your business plan should outline your company's goals, expressed in quantifiable metrics, such as revenue and growth rate targets. Describe how you plan to measure success and track progress towards your goals. Use specific milestones and key performance indicators (KPIs) to maintain focus and motivate your team.

In conclusion, developing a business plan should be a priority for any entrepreneur. The process requires a lot of effort and research, but the rewards are significant. By following the tips outlined above, you can create a comprehensive plan that will not only guide your business but also impress investors and help secure funding to turn your dream into a reality.

CHAPTER 4: OVERCOMING FEAR AND FAILURE

For many aspiring entrepreneurs, fear of failure can be a daunting obstacle that restricts their potential to overcome challenges and succeed in their business ventures. While it's natural to feel some level of anxiety as new entrepreneurs, letting that fear debilitate you can prohibit you from taking the necessary risks to grow your business. Facing and overcoming your fears is essential to achieve success in entrepreneurship. In this chapter, we will discuss overcoming fear and failure in your business endevour.

Understanding common fears associated with entrepreneurship

Entrepreneurship can evoke various fears for many individuals. Fear of failure, fear of financial turbulence, fear of the unknown, fear of rejection, and fear of criticism are some common ones. These fears often stem from uncertainties, and inexperienced entrepreneurs do not know what to expect from pursuing their goals.

It's essential to recognize and understand these fears to overcome them effectively. Fear can also be an excellent motivator if it's met head-on, as it can push you to work harder. But if not addressed, it can become a paralyzing force with negative impacts on personal and business growth.

How to overcome fears and take action

Although fears and worries are natural when starting a business, it's crucial to overcome them to surpass your limitations and strive for success. Here are some tips to help you move past these fears and take action:

1. Identify your fears:

Acknowledge and identify your fears. Assess their legitimacy and consider how you can break them down into smaller, manageable tasks. For instance, if your fear is the lack of experience, you can invest additional time in research to expand your knowledge.

2. Create a plan:

Perhaps you fear the possibility of failing. Therefore, it's important to plan for failure. This way, you are prepared if the worst-case scenario unfolds. Planning enables you to think critically and realistically about potential outcomes.

3. Seek advice:

Mentorship from a seasoned entrepreneur can be invaluable when overcoming fears. A mentor can guide you through the challenges and serve as a sounding board to discuss your concerns.

4. Practice self-care:

Create time to relax, eat healthily, exercise and stay present in your relationships. Doing activities that refresh your mind can help you cope with uncertainties.

5. Get comfortable with the uncomfortable:

Finally, push yourself out of your comfort zone regularly.

Pursuing personal growth is often uncomfortable, and embracing this fact can help you become more tolerant of ambiguity and discomfort.

Dealing with failure and learning from mistakes

Failures are inevitable in entrepreneurship but are also essential in the learning and development process. It's vital to view failures and mistakes as learning opportunities and not as the end of the road. Some entrepreneurs' success stories began with failures before they reached their breakthrough moments. However, it's equally important to understand what causes these failures and why.

Entrepreneurs must adopt a mindset that embraces failure, understands its contributing factors, and provides a strategy for learning from failures and improving their processes. Here are a few tips to keep in mind when dealing with failures:

1. Identify your feelings:

Initially, it's okay to feel upset, disappointed, or frustrated after experiencing a failure. Identify those feelings clearly, and understand how they're affecting your behavior. Acknowledging feelings shows you're in touch with your experience, and that you're not denying it.

2. Analyze the situation:

After identifying your feelings, it's important to assess the reason for the failure. Take a step back and analyze the situation objectively, identify what went wrong and why it went wrong.

3. Create action steps:

The next step is to develop a strategy for addressing the problem. Break the solution process down into smaller manageable steps with specific timelines. Retrofitting and adjusting potential mistakes is equally important to avoid problems.

4. Use feedback and criticism:

Many entrepreneurs encounter criticism and feedback during their initial stages, sometimes even before launching the business. Instead of taking these as negative, use criticism constructively to learn, where needed.

5. Learn from others:

Finally, read other entrepreneurs' stories and learn about their struggles and achievements, listen to their advice, and find a community of people with similar experiences.

Importance of resilience in entrepreneurship

Resilience is the ability to bounce back from difficult situations, setbacks, and failures. It's about being able to acknowledge problems, seek solutions, and maintain persistence in difficult times. As an entrepreneur, it's imperative to understand how to adapt to adversity and to see failures as progress instead of setbacks.

Entrepreneurial failure can result in negative consequences, such as financial stress and mental health struggles. Still, with resilience, entrepreneurs can learn to manage and mitigate those risks. Here are some suggestions for cultivating resilience:

1. Focus on self-care:

Engage in activities that are emotionally and mentally therapeutic, such as meditation or yoga. These can help rejuvenate you and offer clarity in challenging times.

2. Surround yourself with positivity:

Surrounding yourself with positive, supportive people can help boost your confidence levels during difficult times. Having a business mentor, a good life coach or a group of entrepreneurs that you can share similar experiences with can enable collective learning.

3. Develop a positive mindset:

A positive attitude can help you stay resilient in the face of adverse circumstances. Having a mindset that is open to learning, that views failures as lessons, is an effective way of maintaining a positive outlook.

4. Learn to be adaptable:

In volatile environments, lessons and processes require retrofitting. Being adaptable to change can save a business, mitigate downturns and an emphatic skill entrepreneurs must have.

5. Cultivate tenacity:

Lastly, keep trying even when you're experiencing setbacks. Entrepreneurship is not an overnight accomplishment. By persevering through difficulties, you will acquire the persistence that is needed to achieve success.

Learning from successful entrepreneurs who have faced failure

Finally, it's essential to study successful entrepreneurs' failures and how they overcame them as many entrepreneurs tackle common challenges. Learning about the best practices and business strategies that led to their successes to help you establish your game plan. Studying these individuals can lend the required perspective to view failure as necessary for growth.

Steve Jobs, for example, was fired from Apple Inc. early on in his career, a company he helped found. He later rejoined Apple and led the rapid development and growth of Apple products. Jobs once stated, "I am convinced that the only thing that kept me going was that I loved what I did. You've got to find what you love." His determination, love, and streak of resilience were critical ingredients in his success.

Arianna Huffington, founder of Huffington Post, had a difficult time establishing her media company. Confronted with skepticism and joblessness, she kept working with her team and refined her approach until the Huffington Post finally became a mainstream new source. A quote from Arianna: "Fearlessness is like a muscle. I know from my own life that the more I exercise it, the more natural it becomes to not let my fears run me."

Another example of an entrepreneur who exhibits the resilience to overcome failure is Jack Ma, the Chinese business magnate who founded Alibaba. Before he started Alibaba, his early internet ventures failed, including an initial foray into e-commerce. However, he kept at it and learned from his failures, quoting "If you don't give up, you still have a chance. And when you are small, you have to be very focused and rely on your brain, not your strength."

In conclusion, aspiring entrepreneurs must realize that fear and failure are natural occurrences that come with business ownership. By acknowledging and addressing these fears, entrepreneurs can better focus on building resilient and successful companies. Adopting resilience-building strategies, analyzing past accomplishments, and exercising faith and persistence will provide challenging, yet manageable paths, towards success.

CHAPTER 5: NETWORKING AND BUILDING RELATIONSHIPS

Entrepreneurship can be a lonely journey. However, building strong relationships and creating a supportive network is essential for business success. Entrepreneurs who neglect to build relationships with peers, partners, mentors, and other supportive communities are missing out on significant benefits.

Networking and relationship-building are essential components of entrepreneurship because they can provide critical resources, including referrals, partnerships, funding opportunities, and industry insights. In this chapter, we will discuss the importance of networking and relationship-building, strategies for building a strong professional network, leveraging social media for networking, developing a personal brand, collaborating with other entrepreneurs, importance of maintaining relationships, attending conferences and industry events, and how to overcome shyness and social anxiety.

Importance of networking and relationship-building

Relationships are fundamental to entrepreneurship. They help establish trust, support, and increase the chances of success.

Networking allows you to connect, brainstorm, and share with other entrepreneurs facing similar challenges or opportunities. Through networking, you can meet mentors, potential customers, partners, and investors who can help your business grow.

Strategies for building a strong professional network

Building relationships takes time and effort. Here are some strategies to help you build a strong professional network.

- ❖ Attend networking events – Whether online or in-person, attending industry events, conferences, and meetups are incredible avenues to connect with other entrepreneurs.

- ❖ Join industry associations – Joining industry associations can help you expand your network and gain insights into industry trends, regulations, and best practices.

- ❖ Get involved in online communities – Engaging with online communities such as LinkedIn groups, Facebook groups, or forums can lead to valuable connections and opportunities for collaboration.

- ❖ Find a mentor – Seek out successful entrepreneurs who are willing to share their experiences, knowledge, and connections.

- ❖ Focus on quality over quantity – Building relationships should not be about the number of people you know, but rather the depth of relationships that you build.

Leveraging social media for networking

In today's digital age, social media is a powerful tool for networking and building relationships. LinkedIn is the most popular platform among entrepreneurs to connect with other professionals in their industry. Here are some tips for leveraging social media for networking:

❖ Optimize your LinkedIn profile – Make sure your profile is complete and showcases your background, skills, and experiences.

❖ Engage with content – Comment and share industry-related content to spark conversations and increase visibility.

❖ Use LinkedIn groups – Join LinkedIn groups related to your industry or interests, and participate in discussions.

❖ Connect with influencers – Identify thought leaders and influencers in your industry and connect with them.

❖ Share your passion – Use social media to share your passion project, company culture, or expert insights.

Developing a personal brand

Your personal brand is how you present yourself to others. Entrepreneurs who cultivate a strong personal brand can differentiate themselves from their competitors and build credibility within their industry. Here are some tips to develop your personal brand:

❖ Define your story – Develop a unique brand story that showcases your experiences, expertise, and values.

❖ Choose a great profile photo – Your profile picture should be professional, high quality, and reflect your brand personality.

❖ Create consistent content – Consistent and valuable content can help position you as an expert and attract like-minded individuals to your brand.

❖ Focus on your expertise – Showcase your specialized skills and knowledge to differentiate yourself from the competition.

Collaborating with other entrepreneurs

Collaborating with other entrepreneurs can accelerate your startup's success. Collaboration helps leverage resources, increase the visibility of your business, and create opportunities for growth. Here are some ways entrepreneurs can collaborate:

❖ Partner with other startups – Look for startups with similar goals and customers to collaborate on projects, events, or marketing campaigns.

❖ Create affiliate programs – Create mutually beneficial relationships by partnering with other startups to promote each other's products or services.

❖ Host industry events – Organize events that bring industry professionals together to discuss current trends, opportunities, and challenges.

❖ Joint venture – Collaborate with other businesses on projects with the intent of splitting the rewards and risks.

Importance of maintaining relationships

Relationships require consistent effort and nurture to be successful. Maintaining relationships is vital as it can lead to future business opportunities, referrals, and collaborations. Here are some ways entrepreneurs can maintain relationships:

❖ Regular communication – Consistent communication with your network via email, phone, or social media can help build strong relationships and keep them going.

❖ Personalize your communication – Customize your communication to make it meaningful to your audience and show that you are invested in the relationship.

❖ Add value – Provide value to your network by sharing industry news, insights, and resources that can help them in their businesses.

❖ Show appreciation – Take time to appreciate your network by showing gratitude for their support and efforts.

Overcoming shyness and social anxiety

Networking and relationship-building can be challenging for entrepreneurs who are shy or have social anxiety. However, networking skills are essential to entrepreneurship, and with practice, anyone can master them. Here are some tips to overcome shyness and social anxiety:

❖ Prepare for events – Plan ahead for events by researching attendees and preparing conversation starters to ease nervousness.

❖ Take baby steps – Start small by attending smaller events and gradually work your way up to bigger events.

❖ Focus on others – Focus on others' strengths and listen carefully to their experiences, which will help you keep the conversation going.

❖ Be yourself – Don't try to be someone you are not – be authentic and genuine.

Attending conferences and industry events

Attending conferences and industry events can provide entrepreneurs with opportunities to meet new people, gain industry insights, and explore partnership possibilities. Here are some tips for making the most of conferences and events:

❖ Set goals – Identify your goals before attending the event, such as the number of connections you want to establish or the insights you want to gain.

❖ Plan ahead – Research the event's speakers, attendees, and schedule, which can help you plan which events to attend.

❖   Follow up – Follow up with attendees after the event via email or social media to continue the conversation and build relationships.

Conclusion

Networking and relationship-building are critical to the success of every entrepreneur. Building a supportive professional network can provide entrepreneurs with the necessary resources, insights, and guidance to navigate the challenges of entrepreneurship. By following the tips and strategies shared in this chapter, entrepreneurs can create a strong and long-lasting network, eliminate shyness and social anxiety, and make the most of conferences and industry events.

CHAPTER 6: FUNDING YOUR BUSINESS

One of the most important aspects of starting a business is finding the necessary funding to turn your ideas into reality. Without funding, it can be extremely difficult to get your business off the ground. In this chapter, we will discuss the different sources of funding available to entrepreneurs and share tips on how to secure the funds you need to succeed.

Sources of Funding

One of the first decisions you will need to make when seeking funding is whether to self-fund or raise capital from external sources. Self-funding, also known as bootstrapping, involves using your own savings or personal credit to finance your business. While this can be a good option for those who have the necessary funds, it can also limit your business's growth potential. External sources of funding include:

❖ Friends and Family: One of the most common sources of funding for entrepreneurs is friends and family. This can be a good option for those who are just starting out and need a small amount of capital to get their business off the ground. However, it is important to approach friends and family with caution as personal relationships can become strained if the business does not succeed.

❖ Bank Loans: Banks offer a variety of loans, including

business loans, personal loans, and lines of credit. To qualify for a bank loan, you will need to have a good credit score and a solid business plan. The downside to bank loans is that they can be difficult to obtain and often require collateral.

❖ Crowdfunding: Crowdfunding has become a popular way to raise capital for businesses. With crowdfunding, you can raise funds from a large number of people through online platforms such as Kickstarter and IndieGoGo. However, it can be difficult to stand out among the thousands of other campaigns seeking funding.

❖ Angel Investors: Angel investors are wealthy individuals or groups who invest their own funds in early-stage businesses in exchange for equity. They can be a good source of funding for those who are unable to secure funding through other means, but it is important to be prepared to give up a portion of your company in exchange for their investment.

❖ Venture Capitalists: Venture capitalists are professional investors who invest in high-growth startups in exchange for equity. They typically invest larger sums of money than angel investors and are more selective in the companies they choose to invest in.

Developing a Financial Plan

Before seeking funding, it is important to develop a financial plan for your business. A financial plan should include a budget, projected income statements, and cash flow projections. This plan will help you determine how much funding you need and where you can allocate the funds.

When developing your financial plan, consider the following:

❖ Start-up costs: Identify the costs associated with starting your business, including equipment, office space, legal fees, and marketing expenses.

❖ Operating expenses: Identify the costs associated with running your business, including rent, salaries, and inventory.

❖ Revenue projections: Estimate your revenue based on your sales forecast and market research.

❖ Cash flow projections: Determine how much cash your business will generate and when it will be generated. This will help you determine when you will need funding and how much you will need.

Preparing for Investor Pitches

When seeking funding from investors, it is important to prepare a pitch that showcases your business's potential. Your pitch should include:

❖ Executive summary: A brief overview of your business, including your mission statement, target market, and products or services.

❖ Marketing strategy: A detailed explanation of your marketing strategy, including how you plan to reach your target market and differentiate yourself from competitors.

❖ Financials: A detailed breakdown of your financial plan, including start-up costs, revenue projections, and cash flow projections.

❖ Team: An overview of your team's experience and expertise.

❖ Ask: A clear ask for funding and a statement on how the investor will benefit from investing in your business.

It is important to practice your pitch and be prepared to answer questions from potential investors.

Tips for Managing Finances

Managing finances is critical to the success of any business. Here are some tips to help you manage your finances:

❖ Keep track of expenses: Keep a record of all your business expenses to ensure you stay within your budget.

❖ Separate business and personal finances: Keep your personal finances separate from your business finances to avoid confusion and to simplify bookkeeping.

❖ Monitor cash flow: Monitor your cash flow regularly to ensure you have enough funds to cover your expenses.

❖ Hire an accountant: Consider hiring an accountant to help you manage your finances and keep your accounting books in order.

❖ Use financial software: Consider using financial software to help you manage your finances more efficiently.

In conclusion, funding is an essential component of entrepreneurship. Without sufficient funding, it can be difficult to get a business off the ground and achieve success. By understanding the different sources of funding available and developing a strong financial plan, entrepreneurs can increase their chances of securing the necessary funds. It is also important to manage finances carefully to ensure the long-term success of the business.

CHAPTER 7: TIME MANAGEMENT AND PRODUCTIVITY

As an entrepreneur, your time is one of your most valuable assets. How you use it can determine the success or failure of your business. Successful entrepreneurs are known for their time management strategies and their ability to prioritize tasks effectively. In this chapter, we will explore the importance of time management in entrepreneurship and provide strategies to help you increase productivity.

Importance of Time Management in Entrepreneurship

One of the biggest challenges for entrepreneurs is managing their time effectively. With so many tasks to complete, it can be overwhelming to decide where to start and how to get everything done. Time management is essential for several reasons:

❖ Increased Productivity: Effective time management can increase productivity and performance. When you manage your time well, you can focus on the most important tasks and complete them efficiently.

❖ Reduced Stress: Poor time management can lead to increased stress levels, which can negatively impact your health and well-being. Effective time management reduces stress levels and helps you maintain a healthy work-life balance.

❖ Improved Decision Making: When you manage your time effectively, you have more time to think and make better decisions. You are less likely to make rushed decisions that can lead to mistakes and failures.

Strategies for Prioritizing Tasks and Managing Time Effectively

Now that we have discussed the importance of time management let's look at some strategies to help you prioritize tasks and manage your time effectively.

❖ Create a Daily Schedule: Start by creating a daily schedule. This should include all tasks and appointments. List the most important tasks first and allocate specific times for each task. Use a planner or a tool such as Google Calendar to keep track of your schedule.

❖ Prioritize Tasks: Prioritize tasks based on their importance and urgency. Use a system such as the Eisenhower Matrix (a productivity tool that helps you prioritize tasks by urgency and importance) to help you decide which tasks to tackle first.

❖ Avoid Distractions: Distractions can derail your schedule and reduce productivity. Avoid distractions by turning off notifications, closing unnecessary tabs, and minimizing interruptions.

❖ Outsourcing Tasks to Increase Productivity: As an entrepreneur, you may feel the need to do everything yourself, but this can lead to burnout. Consider outsourcing tasks that are not your core competencies. Outsourcing can include hiring contractors or a virtual assistant to help free up your time.

❖ Taking Breaks and Self-Care: It's essential to take breaks and prioritize self-care. Schedule time for lunch breaks, exercise, and breaks for meditation or mindfulness. When you take care of yourself, you can increase productivity and reduce stress levels.

❖ Time Management Tools and Apps: Take advantage of time management tools and apps that can help you manage your time more effectively. Examples include Trello, Asana, and RescueTime.

❖ Building a Productive Routine: Develop a productive routine that includes a consistent sleeping schedule, exercise, and a set morning routine. Having a routine helps create structure and increases productivity throughout the day.

Conclusion

Time management is crucial for entrepreneurs to be successful. By understanding the importance of prioritizing tasks, avoiding distractions, and outsourcing non-core competencies, entrepreneurs can build a productive and effective business. It's all about finding the right methods that work for you. Efficient time management can reduce stress, increase productivity, and improve performance. Remember to take the time to take care of yourself and to consistently evaluate and adjust your schedule to fit the needs of your business and personal life.

CHAPTER 8: BUILDING A STRONG TEAM

Building a successful business requires more than just having a great idea. It takes a team of talented individuals who share a common vision and work together to achieve the organization's goals. Building a strong team is one of the essential tasks of every entrepreneur. In this chapter, we will discuss the process of building a strong team and maintaining a company culture that fosters creativity, growth, and mutual respect.

Importance of a Strong Team

Having a strong team is critical to the success of any business venture. A strong team can help you achieve your business goals faster and more efficiently. An effective team brings together individuals who have different skill sets, experiences, and perspectives, making it easier to accomplish complex tasks.

A strong team is also essential for building and maintaining a positive company culture. A supportive company culture can help you to retain top talent and attract new employees that share your values and vision. A strong team can also help to spread positive energy and enthusiasm throughout your organization.

Finding the Right People for Your Team

As an entrepreneur, your success depends largely on the people you bring into your organization. It's essential to find the right people for your team who can help you achieve your goals and bring your vision to life. Here are some tips for finding the right people for your team:

- ❖ Define Your Needs: Before you start hiring, define the roles you need to fill in your organization. Think carefully about the skills, experiences, and personalities needed for each role.

- ❖ Look for Talent: Look for candidates who have the skills and experience needed for the role, but also consider their work ethic, communication skills, and cultural fit.

- ❖ Cast a Wide Net: Don't limit your search to local candidates. Consider remote workers, freelancers, and people from other areas who can work effectively as part of your team.

- ❖ Use Social Media: Social media platforms like LinkedIn, Twitter, and Facebook can be powerful tools for finding and connecting with potential hires.

Developing a Company Culture

A strong company culture is essential for long-term success. A supportive and positive company culture can attract top talent and reduce employee turnover. Here are some tips for developing a company culture that fosters creativity, growth, and mutual respect:

- ❖ Lead by Example: As a leader, your actions shape your company culture. Set the tone for the organization by modeling the behaviors and values you want to see in your team.

- ❖ Communicate Your Vision: Share your vision for the organization with your team regularly. Make sure everyone understands the mission, values, and goals of the company.

- ❖ Foster Collaboration: Encourage teamwork by creating a

space where employees can work together and share ideas. This might include open office spaces, video conferencing tools, and collaborative project management software.

❖ Encourage Learning: Provide opportunities for your team to learn and grow. This could include attending conferences, taking courses, or attending workshops.

Leadership and Management Skills

As an entrepreneur, you will need to develop strong leadership and management skills to build and maintain a strong team. Here are some tips for becoming an effective leader:

❖ Lead by Example: As a leader, you need to set an example for your team to follow. This means modeling the behaviors and values you want to see in your team.

❖ Communicate Clearly: Good communication is essential for effective leadership. Be clear and concise when giving directives, and be receptive to feedback from your team.

❖ Delegate Effectively: Delegation is an essential skill for every leader. Identify the strengths and weaknesses of each team member and delegate tasks accordingly.

❖ Encourage Innovation: Foster a culture of innovation by encouraging employees to take risks and experiment with new ideas.

Overcoming Common Team Challenges

Building a strong team isn't always easy. Even the best teams can face challenges from time to time. Here are some common team challenges and tips for overcoming them:

❖ Communication Breakdowns: Miscommunication is a common source of conflict in teams. Encourage open and honest communication, and be clear about expectations and responsibilities.

❖   Personality Conflicts: People don't always get along, and personality conflicts can be a source of stress and tension in the workplace. Encourage team members to be respectful and empathetic towards one another.

❖   Burnout: Overworking can lead to burnout, which can negatively affect team morale and productivity. Encourage work-life balance and provide support for employees who may be struggling with stress.

❖   Skill Gaps: Sometimes, team members may lack the skills needed to perform certain tasks effectively. Provide training and support to help fill in skill gaps.

Retaining Top Talent

Retention is an essential aspect of building a strong team. Losing valuable employees can be costly and negatively impact team morale. Here are some tips for retaining top talent:

1. Provide Growth Opportunities: Provide opportunities for your team members to learn and grow. This could include attending conferences, taking courses, or attending workshops.

2. Offer Competitive Compensation: Make sure your compensation package is competitive and reflects the value your team members bring to the organization.

3. Provide a Supportive Work Environment: A supportive work environment is essential for retaining top talent. Encourage work-life balance and provide support for employees who may be struggling with stress.

4. Recognition Programs: Recognize and reward team members who demonstrate exceptional performance. This could include bonuses, promotions, or public recognition.

Conclusion

Building a strong team is essential for the success of any business venture. A well-functioning team can bring diverse perspectives and skill sets to the table, making it easier to achieve complex tasks. As an entrepreneur, it's essential to nurture a supportive company culture that fosters creativity, growth, and mutual respect. By hiring the right people, developing strong leadership and management skills, and creating opportunities for growth and innovation, you can build a successful business that stands the test of time.

CHAPTER 9: MARKETING AND BRANDING

Marketing and branding are two essential components of running a successful business. They both relate to how your company is perceived by the public and can greatly influence the success of your business. Marketing is the process of promoting and selling your products or services while branding is the creation of a company's identity. Together, they create a strong foundation for your business and can help you build a loyal customer base. In this chapter, we will discuss the importance of branding in entrepreneurship, developing a marketing strategy, and measuring marketing success.

Establishing a Brand Identity

Branding is the process of creating a unique identity for your company. A strong brand identity can help differentiate your business from competitors, create a sense of trust and loyalty with customers, and increase brand recognition. Your brand identity should encompass all aspects of your business, from your logo to your marketing messages to the customer experience.

Developing a brand identity starts with defining your brand's values and personality. This includes determining your brand's mission, vision, and goals. Your brand's values should align with the vision of your business and should be reflected in every aspect of your company. A consistent brand message is essential for establishing credibility with your audience.

The visual elements of your brand, such as your logo and color scheme, are also important components of your brand identity. These should be designed to reflect your brand's personality and values. Your logo should be iconic and easily recognizable. The color scheme and typography should also be consistent across all marketing materials.

Creating a Marketing Strategy

Your marketing strategy is the plan you create to reach your target audience and communicate the message of your brand. The goal of marketing is to generate leads, make sales, and ultimately grow your business. A successful marketing strategy involves understanding your target audience and reaching them through the right channels.

To create a marketing strategy, it's important to first identify your target customer. This includes demographic information such as age, gender, and location, as well as psychographic information such as interests, values, and lifestyle. Knowing your target customer will help you create messages that resonate with them and tailor your marketing efforts to their needs.

Once you know your target customer, you can create messaging specific to their needs and interests. This messaging should be reflected in all marketing materials, including social media posts, email marketing campaigns, and advertising.

In addition to messaging, it's important to choose the right channels to reach your target audience. This may include social media platforms, email marketing, or traditional advertising methods such as print and television ads. Each channel has unique benefits and requires a different approach to marketing.

Leveraging social media for marketing is a key component of

modern marketing strategies. Social media platforms such as Facebook, Instagram, and Twitter allow businesses to connect with their audience in a more personal way. Through social media, you can share your brand message, engage with customers, and build your brand's awareness.

Creating Exceptional Customer Experiences

Creating exceptional customer experiences goes hand in hand with successful marketing and branding. A positive customer experience can greatly impact a customer's perception of your brand and lead to repeat business and referrals.

To create a positive customer experience, it's important to understand your customer's needs and expectations. This includes understanding their pain points and addressing them in your marketing messaging. It also includes providing exceptional customer service throughout the sales process and after the sale is complete.

Personalization is another important component of creating a positive customer experience. Customers expect businesses to understand their unique needs and preferences. This can include personalizing marketing messages and offering personalized product recommendations.

The customer experience doesn't just end after the sale is complete. It's important to follow up with customers to ensure their satisfaction and address any issues they may have. Collecting customer feedback is also important for improving your customer experience and identifying areas for improvement.

Measuring Marketing Success

Measuring the success of your marketing strategy is essential for improving your approach and growing your business. There are numerous metrics you can track, including website traffic, conversion rates, and social media engagement. These metrics provide insights into how your marketing efforts are performing and how you can improve your strategy for better results.

One important metric to track is your return on investment (ROI). This measures the revenue generated from your marketing efforts compared to the cost of those efforts. Tracking your ROI can help you determine which marketing channels are most effective and where to focus your marketing efforts for the best results.

Another important metric to track is customer lifetime value (CLV). This measures the total revenue generated over the lifetime of a customer. Measuring CLV can help you identify your most valuable customers and how to retain them.

In addition to these metrics, it's important to collect customer feedback through surveys and other means. This feedback can help you understand how customers perceive your brand and where you can improve your marketing and customer experience.

Conclusion

Marketing and branding are critical components of building a successful business. Building a strong brand identity, developing a targeted marketing strategy, and creating exceptional customer experiences can greatly impact how your business is perceived and its success. By measuring your marketing success and collecting customer feedback, you can continually improve your marketing efforts and build a stronger brand.

CHAPTER 10: INNOVATING AND STAYING COMPETITIVE

Entrepreneurship involves taking risks and thinking outside of the box. It is essential for entrepreneurs to innovate if they want to stay competitive in the market. Customers are always looking for unique and innovative products and services, and entrepreneurs who can consistently deliver will be the ones to succeed. In this chapter, we will discuss the importance of innovation in entrepreneurship and how you can stay ahead of the competition while maintaining your edge.

Identifying market trends

Innovation starts with identifying market trends. An entrepreneur who can identify a trend early and pivot their business to take advantage of it will be more successful than one who is late to the game. Keeping tabs on what your competitors are doing is crucial, but it's also important to look for new ideas outside of your industry.

Staying ahead of the competition

It's not enough to just identify market trends; you have to stay ahead of the competition. One way to do this is by continually updating your offerings to keep up with changing customer needs. Keep your finger on the pulse of what your customers want and need, and make changes accordingly. Don't be afraid to take risks and try new things.

Incorporating customer feedback

Customer feedback is a valuable tool for innovation. Listening to what your customers have to say can help you identify areas for improvement and new opportunities. Make it a habit to regularly gather feedback from your customers and use it to guide your business decisions. This will keep you ahead of the competition and help you create products and services that resonate with your customers.

Encouraging creativity and experimentation

Entrepreneurs who encourage creativity and experimentation among their team members are more likely to come up with innovative ideas. Don't be afraid to give your team members the freedom to experiment and try new things. Encourage out-of-the-box thinking and reward team members who come up with innovative ideas. This will help you stay ahead of the competition and create products and services that stand out from the crowd.

Importance of adaptability

One of the most important traits an entrepreneur can have is adaptability. Markets change, trends come and go, and customer needs evolve. Entrepreneurs who can adapt quickly to these changes and pivot their business accordingly will be more successful than those who don't. Be open to change and always be ready to pivot your business to take advantage of new opportunities.

Overcoming fear of change

Change can be scary, but it's essential for innovation and staying competitive. Entrepreneurs who are afraid of change will be left behind. Overcoming the fear of change takes practice and a willingness to take risks. Surround yourself with team members who are open to change and encourage them to speak up when they have ideas for innovation.

Learning from successful innovators

There is much to learn from successful innovators. Take the time to study successful entrepreneurs who have made a name for themselves by innovating. Look for common threads and try to apply those lessons to your own business. Don't be afraid to reach out to successful entrepreneurs and ask for advice. Many successful entrepreneurs are happy to share their knowledge with others.

Conclusion

Innovation is essential for staying competitive in today's fast-paced business world. Entrepreneurs who can identify market trends, stay ahead of the competition, incorporate customer feedback, encourage creativity and experimentation, and adapt to changes in the market will be the ones who succeed. Overcoming the fear of change and learning from successful innovators will help you develop the mindset you need to stay ahead of the game.

CHAPTER 11:
MANAGING RISK AND UNCERTAINTY

Risk is inevitable in any business venture. Entrepreneurs need to take calculated risks to achieve success. However, they also need to manage risk and overcome uncertainty associated with entrepreneurship. Risk management is about identifying potential threats and analyzing potential outcomes of those threats. By doing this, entrepreneurs can develop a risk management plan to reduce the negative impact of risk on their businesses.

Uncertainty is also a significant factor that entrepreneurs have to face. They need to be prepared for unexpected events and adapt to changes in the business environment. They need to develop resilience to cope with uncertainty and maintain a positive outlook.

Understanding Risk in Entrepreneurship

Risk is unavoidable in entrepreneurship. It is because entrepreneurs face many unknowns and uncertainties associated with the market, competition, finances, and other factors. Entrepreneurs have to make decisions based on incomplete information. They need to determine the level of risk they want to take and how to manage that risk.

Entrepreneurs have to identify potential threats to their business by conducting a risk assessment. A risk assessment is a process of identifying potential threats and analyzing their potential impact on the business. It helps entrepreneurs develop a risk management plan to mitigate potential risks and minimize the negative impact of those risks.

Developing a Risk Management Plan

A risk management plan helps entrepreneurs manage risks associated with their businesses. It provides a framework for identifying, assessing, and mitigating potential risks. It is essential to develop a risk management plan to reduce the negative impact of risk on the business.

The first step to developing a risk management plan is to identify potential threats. Entrepreneurs can use various methods, such as brainstorming, to identify potential risks. They can also use tools such as SWOT analysis, PEST analysis, and Porter's Five Forces analysis to identify potential threats.

Once entrepreneurs have identified potential threats, they need to analyze the potential impact of those threats on their business. They should determine the likelihood of each threat occurring and the potential impact of each threat on their business. They can use techniques such as scenario analysis, sensitivity analysis, and decision trees to analyze potential outcomes.

After analyzing potential risks, entrepreneurs need to develop a risk management strategy. The strategy should include measures to mitigate potential risks and minimize the negative impact of those risks. Entrepreneurs should prioritize risks based on their impact on the business and the likelihood of occurrence. They should also allocate resources to implement the risk management strategy.

Managing Uncertainty

Uncertainty is also a significant factor that entrepreneurs have to face. They need to be prepared for unexpected events and adapt to changes in the business environment. They need to develop resilience to cope with uncertainty and maintain a positive outlook.

There are many ways entrepreneurs can manage uncertainty:

❖ Develop a contingency plan: A contingency plan is a plan of action that an entrepreneur can implement when unexpected events occur. It helps entrepreneurs manage unexpected events and minimize the negative impact of those events.

❖ Diversify the business: Entrepreneurs can diversify their businesses by expanding their products or services or entering new markets. Diversification helps entrepreneurs reduce their dependence on a single product or market, reducing the impact of potential threats.

❖ Stay informed: Entrepreneurs need to stay informed about changes in the business environment, such as changes in regulations, new market trends, and new competitors. This helps them adapt to changes and take advantage of new opportunities.

❖ Build a strong team: A strong team helps entrepreneurs manage unexpected events and adapt to changes in the business environment. Entrepreneurs should hire employees with diverse skills and experience to manage different aspects of their businesses.

❖ Maintain a positive outlook: Maintaining a positive outlook helps entrepreneurs cope with uncertainty and maintain motivation. Entrepreneurs should focus on their long-term vision and stay committed to their goals.

Conclusion

Risk and uncertainty are inevitable in entrepreneurship. Entrepreneurs have to take risks to achieve success, but they also need to manage those risks and cope with uncertainty. Developing a risk management plan helps entrepreneurs identify potential threats and mitigate risks. Managing uncertainty requires entrepreneurs to develop resilience and maintain a positive outlook.

Entrepreneurs should be prepared for unexpected events and adapt to changes in the business environment. They should stay informed about changes in regulations, market trends, and competitors. They should build a strong team to manage different aspects of their businesses and focus on their long-term vision. By managing risks and uncertainty, entrepreneurs can increase their chances of success and achieve their goals.

CHAPTER 12:
DEVELOPING A
GLOBAL MINDSET

In today's modern age of business, having a global mindset is extremely important for the success of any entrepreneur. No longer are businesses just focused on their local or national markets; current technology and communication methods have made it easier for entrepreneurs to work with anyone across the world.

To develop a global mindset, entrepreneurs must start by thinking globally. This means keeping in mind that different cultures and countries have different business practices, economic systems, and political structures that can significantly impact how a business operates. Entrepreneurs must study these differences, understand how they may impact their business, and adapt accordingly.

One way to develop a global mindset is to identify opportunities in international markets. Entrepreneurs must conduct in-depth research and analysis to find opportunities for their products or services from countries they may not have considered before. Depending on the nature of the business, expanding into foreign markets may lead to more revenue, new partnerships, and the opportunity to learn from different business practices.

However, identifying opportunities in international markets is not enough. Entrepreneurs must also learn how to navigate cultural differences and language barriers. This can be done by hiring individuals who are knowledgeable in different languages or cultures to help facilitate communication and improve understanding. It is also essential to learn cultural norms and customs in different parts of the world to avoid any potential misunderstandings or miscommunications.

Developing a global network is also crucial for entrepreneurs. Attending trade fairs or conferences that are relevant to the business can help an entrepreneur meet potential partners and learn more about the global market. Online platforms like LinkedIn and Twitter can also be useful tools for entrepreneurs to connect with professionals in their industry globally. This network can be a great resource for the entrepreneur to get information regarding the market and the ways of doing business in different parts of the world.

Another critical aspect of developing a global mindset is the ability to adapt to different business models. Entrepreneurs must be willing to modify their business models to suit the unique needs of different markets. Therefore, it is crucial to gain an understanding of the different market's economic structure, industry practices, and regulatory environment to tailor their approach accordingly. It's essential always to be open to the possibility of varied business models and practices abroad.

Overcoming fear of the unknown is crucial for developing a global mindset. It might be intimidating at first, to explore new territories or to work in different cultures, but it is essential to keep pushing forward and taking new opportunities. Entrepreneurs must be proactive, take risks, and learn quickly from failures regarding cultural awareness or market suitability. Additionally, they need to acknowledge that things don't always go according to plan, and that continuous learning and adaptation are required even after the initial entry into a new market.

Lastly, developing a global mindset means understanding the importance of learning about different cultures. Besides being aware of the economic or market-related practices in different parts of the world, entrepreneurs must also be sensitive to the cultural practices associated with different regions. This is important because, in many business interactions, understanding cultural norms et cetera can make all the difference in building a meaningful and long-lasting relationship. When you care to learn about your client's culture, it also shows respect and a desire to create a mutually beneficial relationship.

In conclusion, a global mindset is essential for entrepreneurs who wish to succeed in today's globalized world. Opportunities are not limited to local/national markets, and entrepreneurs who can effectively navigate international markets and are sensitive to cultural differences are much more likely to excel. Developing a global mindset takes time and effort but the rewards can be substantial. Entrepreneurs who choose to embrace and explore these new opportunities will see significant growth and create a more lasting impact on their industry.

CHAPTER 13:
ETHICS AND SOCIAL
RESPONSIBILITY

Ethics and social responsibility are key components of any successful business, and it is crucial that entrepreneurs incorporate both into their business strategies early on. The way a business operates has a huge impact on its reputation and the perception consumers have of it.

Importance of Ethical Business Practices

Ethical business practices are essential for building trust with clients, customers, and other stakeholders. Operating ethically means doing the right thing, even when no one is watching. It encompasses values such as honesty, integrity, and responsibility. By implementing ethical practices, a business can avoid legal issues and negative publicity which can result from unethical behavior.

Developing a Code of Ethics

One of the first steps entrepreneurs should take is to develop a code of ethics. This is a document that outlines the values and principles that the business will uphold. The code of ethics should be clear and concise, and communicated effectively to all stakeholders. It should also include a system for reporting any unethical practices.

Balancing Profit and Social Responsibility

It is important for entrepreneurs to balance profit and social responsibility. Consumers are increasingly conscious of the impact their purchases have on the environment and society, and they are more likely to support businesses that demonstrate a commitment to making a positive impact. A business that prioritizes social responsibility can attract and retain customers who share similar values.

Importance of Giving Back to the Community

Entrepreneurs should also consider the impact their business can have on the local community and society as a whole. Giving back to the community can take various forms such as supporting local charities, sponsoring local events, or volunteering. Beyond building goodwill in the community, it can also enhance a business's public image and foster a sense of community within the organization.

Importance of Sustainability

Sustainability has become a buzzword in recent years, but it is more than just a trend. It is a way of operating that aims to minimize negative environmental impacts while maintaining business viability. Sustainable business practices can lead to long-term profitability and a positive environmental impact, making it a win-win approach.

Overcoming Ethical Dilemmas

It is not uncommon for businesses to face ethical dilemmas. Entrepreneurs should be prepared to face difficult decisions that challenge their values and principles. These dilemmas can arise from various circumstances such as conflicts of interest, pressure from stakeholders, or personal beliefs. The key is to have a clear understanding of the business's ethical code and to make decisions that align with those values.

Building a Reputation for Integrity

Integrity is a vital component of any successful business. A business that operates with integrity can build trust among stakeholders and develop long-term relationships. Entrepreneurs should ensure that their actions align with their words and that they deliver on promises. A business that consistently acts with integrity builds a strong reputation and is more likely to attract loyal customers.

Learning from Successful Socially Responsible Businesses

There is much to be learned from successful socially responsible businesses. Entrepreneurs can gain valuable insights from studying businesses that have built successful brands while prioritizing social responsibility. Learning from their successes and setbacks can help entrepreneurs identify strategies to incorporate ethical and socially responsible practices into their business models.

Conclusion

Entrepreneurs who prioritize ethics and social responsibility in their business strategies can build trust and goodwill among stakeholders. By establishing a code of ethics, balancing profit with social responsibility, and incorporating sustainable practices, entrepreneurs can develop a positive reputation for their businesses. Additionally, by giving back to the community and learning from successful socially responsible businesses, entrepreneurs can create positive change and build long-term success.

CHAPTER 14: EMBRACING TECHNOLOGY

In today's fast-paced business world, technology is essential to success. Entrepreneurs must stay up-to-date with the latest advancements in technology to remain competitive in their industry. However, embracing technology can be an intimidating task for many people. In this chapter, we'll explore why technology is critical to entrepreneurship, how it can help streamline business operations, and how to overcome any fear of embracing technology.

The Importance of Technology in Entrepreneurship

Technology has transformed the way we do business. It has made it possible for entrepreneurs to reach a wider audience, automate tasks, and reduce costs. Technology has also created new opportunities for businesses to innovate and grow. From social media to cloud computing, technology has become an integral part of the entrepreneurial journey.

One of the most significant benefits of technology is its ability to streamline business operations. For example, automation software can help reduce the workload on administrative tasks, freeing up time for entrepreneurs to focus on growing their business. Technology can also provide entrepreneurs with real-time data to make informed decisions about their business.

Whether it's tracking website traffic or monitoring customer feedback, technology can provide valuable insights into business performance.

Another benefit of technology is its ability to create a stronger online presence. In today's digital age, having a website and social media presence is critical to reaching potential customers. Entrepreneurs can use social media platforms to engage with their audience, share their brand message, and promote their products or services. Additionally, entrepreneurs can leverage search engine optimization (SEO) to increase their online visibility and attract more visitors to their website.

Overcoming Fear of Technology

Despite the numerous benefits of technology, some entrepreneurs may feel overwhelmed or intimidated by it. The rapidly evolving nature of technology can make it difficult to stay on top of changes and advancements. Additionally, some entrepreneurs may feel like they lack the technical skills necessary to fully embrace technology.

Fortunately, there are several ways to overcome these challenges and begin embracing technology. First, entrepreneurs can start by educating themselves about the technologies relevant to their industry or business. There are numerous resources available online, such as blogs, forums, and online courses, which can provide valuable insights into the latest advancements in technology.

Second, it's important for entrepreneurs to have an open mindset when it comes to technology. Instead of viewing it as a burden or obstacle, entrepreneurs should view technology as an opportunity to innovate and grow their business. By embracing technology, entrepreneurs can gain a competitive edge in their industry and stay ahead of the curve.

Finally, entrepreneurs can seek out the help of experts or

consultants to assist them with implementing technology into their business. Whether it's creating a website or setting up a customer relationship management (CRM) system, there are numerous professionals available who can help entrepreneurs navigate the world of technology.

Incorporating Technology into Business Strategy

Once entrepreneurs have embraced technology, the next step is to incorporate it into their business strategy. One of the best ways to do this is by using technology to automate tasks and streamline business operations. For example, entrepreneurs can use project management software to assign tasks and monitor progress among employees. Similarly, online scheduling tools can help entrepreneurs manage their appointments and meetings more efficiently.

Another way to incorporate technology into business strategy is by creating a strong online presence. This includes developing a website, social media profiles, and online marketing campaigns. By leveraging the power of technology, entrepreneurs can reach a larger audience and attract more customers to their business.

Finally, entrepreneurs should be aware of the importance of cybersecurity. With the rise of technology comes the risk of cyber threats such as hacking and data breaches. It's essential for entrepreneurs to take steps to protect their business from these threats, such as using strong passwords and encryption, regularly updating software, and providing cybersecurity training to employees.

Learning from Successful Tech Entrepreneurs

There are numerous successful tech entrepreneurs who have embraced technology and achieved great success. By learning from their experiences, entrepreneurs can gain valuable insights into how to incorporate technology into their own business strategy.

For example, Jeff Bezos, founder of Amazon, has been a driving force behind the rapid growth of the e-commerce industry. Bezos recognized the power of technology to transform the way we shop and pioneered the use of online sales and shipping to create a seamless customer experience.

Similarly, Elon Musk, founder of SpaceX and Tesla, has revolutionized the way we think about space travel and electric cars. Musk's innovative use of technology has helped him achieve remarkable success in these industries.

In conclusion, embracing technology is essential to success in entrepreneurship. By using it to automate tasks, create a strong online presence, and protect against cyber threats, entrepreneurs can gain a competitive edge and achieve long-term success. Overcoming any fear of technology and embracing its possibilities is a key step to achieving success as an entrepreneur.

CHAPTER 15: DEVELOPING STRONG COMMUNICATION SKILLS

As an entrepreneur, your ability to communicate effectively can make or break your business. From pitching your product to investors and potential customers to leading a team and negotiating deals, effective communication is key to success.

In this chapter, we will explore the importance of developing strong communication skills and provide strategies for improving your communication abilities.

Importance of Communication in Entrepreneurship

Effective communication is critical in entrepreneurship for several reasons:

❖ Building relationships: Successful entrepreneurs know the value of building strong relationships with customers, suppliers, investors, and team members. Effective communication is essential for building trust, establishing rapport, and maintaining positive relationships.

❖ Resolving conflicts: Conflicts are common in business, and resolving them requires effective communication skills. Entrepreneurs who can communicate effectively can navigate conflicts, negotiate solutions, and maintain harmony within their organization.

❖ Communicating your vision: An entrepreneur's vision is only as powerful as their ability to communicate it to others. Effective communication skills are needed to inspire and motivate team members, investors, and customers to share and support your vision.

Strategies for Effective Communication

❖ Active Listening: Listening is a fundamental component of communication. As an entrepreneur, it is essential to listen actively to others and acknowledge their viewpoints, concerns, and feedback. Active listening involves paying attention to the speaker, asking clarifying questions, and repeating what you have heard to show that you understand.

❖ Written Communication: Written communication is just as important as verbal communication. Entrepreneurs need to use proper grammar, punctuation, and tone in their emails, proposals, and other written correspondence.

❖ Nonverbal Communication: Nonverbal communication, such as body language and facial expressions, is a crucial part of effective communication. Entrepreneurs need to be aware of their nonverbal cues and use them to convey sincerity, confidence, and enthusiasm.

❖ Simplify Your Language: Clear and concise language is critical for effective communication. Use simple language when explaining complex ideas to team members, investors, and customers.

❖ Build Rapport: Building rapport with others is essential

for effective communication. Finding common ground and showing interest in others' opinions can lead to more productive communication.

❖   Empathy: Empathy helps you understand someone else's perspective and respond appropriately. As an entrepreneur, empathy can help you build relationships, resolve conflicts, and negotiate solutions.

❖   Public Speaking: Public speaking is a crucial skill for entrepreneurs, whether it's presenting to investors, employees, or customers. Entrepreneurs need to prepare adequately, practice their speech, and engage their audience.

Overcoming Communication Barriers

❖   Cultural Differences: Entrepreneurs who work with people from different cultures may encounter communication barriers. Learning about cultural differences and adapting your communication style can help you avoid misunderstandings.

❖   Language Barriers: Entrepreneurs who work with people who speak a different language may face communication barriers. Using a translator or learning basic phrases in the other language can help overcome language barriers.

❖   Avoid Jargon: Jargon refers to technical language, and it can be a barrier to effective communication. Avoid using jargon, or explain technical terms in simple language to ensure that everyone understands.

❖   Addressing Conflict: Conflict can be a communication barrier, and entrepreneurs need to address it proactively. Using active listening skills, acknowledging the other person's perspective, and finding a compromise can help resolve conflicts.

In Conclusion

Effective communication is vital to the success of any business venture. Entrepreneurs who develop strong communication skills can build relationships, resolve conflicts, and communicate their vision effectively. Using strategies such as active listening, written communication, nonverbal communication, simplifying language, building rapport, and public speaking can help entrepreneurs overcome communication barriers and achieve their goals.

CHAPTER 16: MAINTAINING WORK-LIFE BALANCE

Entrepreneurship can be a highly rewarding journey, but it can also be incredibly demanding. Often, entrepreneurs find themselves working long hours, neglecting personal time, and feeling overwhelmed with stress. Achieving work-life balance is crucial for both their health and the success of their business. In this chapter, we outline strategies for entrepreneurs to maintain a healthy balance between work and personal life.

Strategies for Managing Stress

Stress is a natural part of life, but when it becomes persistent, it can have a significant impact on mental and physical health. As an entrepreneur, there may be days when stress seems to be an inevitable part of your life. However, incorporating certain measures into your daily routine can help minimize stress levels.

The first step in managing stress is identifying its source. Is it a particular work task, financial issues, or personal events? Once you have identified the source of stress, you can develop measures to address it. For example, if you find yourself overwhelmed by a particular deadline, breaking down the task into manageable segments can help minimize the impact of stress.

Incorporating physical activity and exercise is another proven strategy to manage stress levels. Getting regular exercise, even 15 minutes per day, can help reduce stress levels and improve mood. Exercise can be, taking a walk or jog, yoga, or another physical activity you enjoy.

Setting Boundaries

Especially when starting a new business, there can be a tendency for entrepreneurs to neglect their personal life. Setting boundaries can help to ensure that there is a balance between work and personal life.

Setting clear designated work hours, and ensuring that friends and family respect those hours, can help create a healthy work-life balance. It is important to communicate with loved ones about the demands of your job and your aspirations. When everyone is on the same page, there is less risk of misunderstanding or increased stress in personal relationships.

Importance of Self-care

Taking care of yourself is critical to maintaining a healthy work-life balance. Making time for activities that bring joy and relaxation can alleviate stress and improve mental health. Such activities can include anything from reading or pursuing a hobby, to taking a warm bath or setting up a regular skincare routine.

Meditation and mindfulness practices are also great strategies for self-care. Practicing deep breathing, setting aside time for meditation, or incorporating yoga practice into your daily routine can help reduce stress levels and improve focus.

Avoiding Burnout

Entrepreneurship can be highly demanding, as entrepreneurs are often responsible for multiple tasks and wear multiple hats. Overloading oneself with work can cause burnout and negatively impact both personal and professional life.

It is important to take breaks from work to avoid burnout. Taking regular breaks, going on holidays, or setting aside "me-time" can help reduce stress levels, keep focus, and improve overall productivity.

Overcoming Guilt Associated With Taking Time Off

Entrepreneurs often have a driving desire to succeed and self-imposed pressure to work harder, longer hours, and put business first. Taking time away from the business isn't a sign of failure but rather a vital part of maintaining balance.

It's important to remind oneself regularly that taking time off is just as important for productivity and success as working tirelessly. Pre-empting time for rest, recuperation, and personal affairs, helps maintain perspective and reduce stress levels related to feelings of guilt.

Building a Support System

Entrepreneurship can be a lonely experience, especially when facing challenging times. Building a support system of friends, mentors, or other entrepreneurs can help alleviate stress and provide the much-needed support system.

Being part of a supportive community can help entrepreneurs navigate challenges, offer perspectives, and provide connections. Joining a mentorship program, business community groups, or attending conferences and workshops that provide networking opportunities can help build a supportive network.

Prioritizing Personal Relationships

Personal relationships are a crucial element of life, and it's important to maintain them despite the demands of entrepreneurship. Additionally, spending quality time with loved ones has been shown to offer a much-needed respite from the challenges of work, thus improving overall productivity.

Prioritizing personal relationships means setting aside time for friends and family. Simple acts such as sharing meals, going for walks, or engaging in hobbies together can strengthen relationships and offer a much-needed break from work.

In conclusion, entrepreneurs must invest in maintaining a healthy work-life balance to achieve long-term success and maintain good mental, and physical health. It's important to develop strategies that help alleviate stress levels, create boundaries, take time for self-care, avoid burnout, overcome guilt, build a support system, and prioritize personal relationships. These strategies facilitate a healthy balance between work and life, which equates to increased productivity, success, and overall well-being.

CHAPTER 17: MENTORSHIP AND CONTINUOUS LEARNING

Entrepreneurship is a journey that is full of ups and downs. Along the way, everyone needs guidance and support, someone who can help us when we are feeling lost and guide us towards success. That's where mentorship comes in. Finding a mentor can be one of the most important decisions you make as an entrepreneur. They can provide you with valuable insights and advice, offer honest feedback and help you develop your skills and expertise.

Finding a Mentor

The first step to finding a mentor is to define your goals and what you hope to achieve from the mentorship. This will help you determine the qualities you are looking for in a mentor and the specific expertise they should have. Look for someone who has experience in your industry, has achieved the kind of success you hope to achieve and is willing to share their knowledge and expertise with you.

Where to Find a Mentor

There are many sources to find mentors, including professional associations, business incubators, and accelerators, networking events, and social media. Investing time in building a solid network of contacts and connections can help you identify potential mentors. Reach out to industry leaders, successful entrepreneurs, and business owners you admire and ask if they would be willing to mentor you. You can also explore mentorship programs offered by organizations or look for online mentorship platforms.

Developing a Mentor-Mentee Relationship

It's important to establish clear goals and expectations for your mentor-mentee relationship, including the frequency of meetings, communication channels, and the areas you would like your mentor to provide guidance and support. Respect your mentor's time and prepare specific questions and topics to discuss in each session. Remember, your mentor is not there to give you all the answers but to guide you towards finding the answers yourself.

Importance of Continuous Learning

A successful entrepreneur understands the importance of continuous learning. As your business grows and evolves, it is important to stay up-to-date with trends and changes in your industry, learn new skills and techniques, and adapt to new technologies. Continuous learning will not only help you stay ahead of the competition but also provide you with new ideas and opportunities for growth.

Seeking Out Resources for Personal and Professional Growth

There are numerous resources available for entrepreneurs to support their learning and growth. Attend conferences and workshops, read industry publications and books, take online courses and certification programs, and participate in industry-specific meetups or groups. Joining a mastermind group or finding a business coach can also provide valuable guidance and support.

Learning from Successful Entrepreneurs

Success leaves clues, and one of the best ways to learn is by studying successful entrepreneurs. Read biographies, listen to interviews and podcasts, and attend events where successful entrepreneurs are speaking. Learning from their experiences, strategies, and mistakes can help you avoid pitfalls, and inspire you to achieve more.

Importance of Giving Back by Mentoring Others

The most successful entrepreneurs also know the importance of giving back. As you build your success, it is important to pay it forward by helping others on their entrepreneurial journey. Becoming a mentor to other aspiring entrepreneurs can be a rewarding and fulfilling experience. Not only will you be sharing your knowledge and insights, but you will also be investing in the future of your industry and community.

Utilizing Online Learning Resources

In today's digital age, there are also countless online learning resources available. You can take courses on platforms like Udemy or Coursera, participate in webinars and online workshops, and even attend virtual conferences. These resources offer flexible and affordable ways to learn and expand your knowledge.

Conclusion

Mentorship and continuous learning are crucial components of the entrepreneurial mindset. Seeking guidance and support from a mentor can help you navigate the challenges of your entrepreneurial journey and achieve success faster. Investing in continuous learning will help you stay ahead of the competition and adapt to changes in your industry. By sharing your knowledge and mentoring others, you can also give back to the entrepreneurial community and invest in the future of your industry.

CHAPTER 18: SCALING YOUR BUSINESS

You've successfully started your business, and now you're ready to take it to the next level. Scaling your business can be an exciting but challenging endeavor. Before you start to grow, it's essential to make sure that your business is ready for expansion. In this chapter, we'll cover the importance of scalability in entrepreneurship, identifying potential growth opportunities, preparing for growth, managing expansion, building a strong team to support growth, maintaining company culture, developing a growth strategy, and measuring success.

Importance of scalability in entrepreneurship

Scalability is the ability of a business to grow and expand without losing efficiency or profitability. The ability to scale is crucial to the long-term success of a business. A scalable business can take advantage of new opportunities, increase revenue, and expand into new markets. Without scalability, a business may struggle to keep up with growing demand, resulting in lost revenue, reduced efficiencies, and customer dissatisfaction.

Identifying potential growth opportunities

Before you can scale your business, you need to identify potential growth opportunities. This may involve expanding into new markets, launching new products or services, or increasing your customer base. To identify growth opportunities, you need to conduct market research, analyze trends, and understand your target audience. Once you have identified the areas with the most potential for growth, you can start to develop a growth strategy.

Preparing for growth

Scaling a business requires careful planning and preparation. Before you start to grow, you need to make sure that your business is ready for expansion. This may involve upgrading your technology, increasing your production capacity, or hiring new staff. It's essential to ensure that your infrastructure can handle increased demand and that you have the resources to support growth.

Managing expansion

Managing expansion is a critical part of scaling your business. As you grow, you'll need to keep a close eye on your cash flow, manage your inventory, and maintain customer satisfaction. You may need to make adjustments to your business processes or systems as you expand to ensure that your business remains efficient and profitable. It's essential to monitor key performance indicators (KPIs) to track your growth and identify areas for improvement continually.

Building a strong team to support growth

As your business grows, you'll need to build a strong team to support your expansion. Hiring the right people with the skills and expertise you need is crucial to scaling your business successfully. You may need to invest in training and development to prepare your team for growth. It's essential to create a supportive work environment that encourages collaboration, innovation, and growth.

Maintaining company culture

Maintaining company culture is vital to the success of a scaling business. Culture refers to the shared values, beliefs, and behaviors that define the personality of your company. As you grow, it's easy for your company culture to change, so it's essential to be intentional about preserving your values and vision. You can do this by involving your team in the growth process, communicating clearly, and leading by example.

Developing a growth strategy

Developing a growth strategy involves setting goals and objectives, identifying key performance indicators, and developing a plan to achieve your growth targets. Your growth strategy should be based on your market research, trends, and customer insights. It should also consider the strengths and weaknesses of your business, your competition, and any potential challenges or risks.

Measuring success

Measuring success is crucial to scaling your business. You need to track your progress against your growth targets and adjust your strategy, as necessary. Use data to inform your decision-making and identify areas for improvement. Regularly reviewing your KPIs and performance metrics will help you understand how successful your growth strategy has been and where you need to focus your efforts going forward.

In conclusion, scaling your business can be an exciting and challenging process. It requires careful planning, preparation, and execution. By building a strong team, maintaining company culture, and developing a growth strategy based on data and customer insights, you can successfully grow your business and achieve long-term success. Remember to measure your success regularly and adjust your strategy as necessary to ensure that you're on track to achieve your growth targets.

CHAPTER 19: GIVING BACK AND MAKING A DIFFERENCE

As an entrepreneur, it is essential to do something that goes beyond making money. The most successful entrepreneurs understand the importance of giving back and making a difference in the world. This is not just about corporate social responsibility, but about creating a sense of purpose that transcends the business itself.

Identifying Ways to Make a Positive Impact

When thinking about giving back, the first step is to identify areas where you can make a positive impact. This could be through philanthropic giving, volunteering, or other forms of community service. For example, you may choose to support a local charity that aligns with your values or sponsor a program that provides education or training to underprivileged youth.

Another way to make a positive impact is through environmental sustainability. Many companies have adopted eco-friendly practices that not only benefit the environment but also save them money in the long run. For instance, a company could minimize its carbon footprint by reducing energy consumption, encouraging recycling, or minimizing the use of plastic products.

Importance of Corporate Social Responsibility

Corporate social responsibility (CSR) is a business approach that emphasizes the importance of making positive contributions to society. It involves taking into account the environmental, social, and ethical impacts of business decisions. This may include investing in community development, employee volunteering programs, or environmental sustainability efforts.

By taking a CSR approach, businesses can build stronger relationships with stakeholders and gain a competitive advantage. Consumers are becoming increasingly aware of the social and environmental impact of the products and services they buy. Companies that prioritize CSR are more likely to attract and retain customers who value these values.

Philanthropic Giving

Philanthropic giving involves donating money or resources to a charitable cause. Many successful entrepreneurs have made significant donations to causes close to their hearts. For example, Bill Gates, the co-founder of Microsoft, has donated millions of dollars to global health initiatives through his foundation.

When considering philanthropic giving, it is important to find a cause that aligns with your values and interests. You may choose to support a local charity or a global cause. It is important to research organizations before making a donation to ensure that your money will be put to good use. You may also choose to donate resources such as time or expertise to support a cause you care about.

Volunteering and Community Service

Volunteering and community service involve giving your time and expertise to support a cause or organization. This is an excellent way to make a positive impact on your community and build relationships with like-minded individuals.

Volunteering can take on many forms, such as organizing a fundraising event, mentoring youth, or providing support for a non-profit organization. By volunteering, you can learn new skills, build your network, and gain a sense of fulfillment that goes beyond financial success.

Importance of Creating a Sense of Purpose

Creating a sense of purpose is essential for entrepreneurs who want to make a difference in the world. This goes beyond just making money or achieving business goals. It is about identifying your values and passions and finding ways to use your business skills to impact others positively.

By creating a sense of purpose, entrepreneurs can motivate themselves and their teams to work towards a common goal. This can lead to better employee retention, stronger customer relationships, and a more meaningful brand.

Learning from Successful Socially Responsible Businesses

Many successful companies have built their brand around social responsibility and making a positive impact. For example, Ben & Jerry's is known for its progressive social values and its support of causes such as racial justice and climate change.

By learning from socially responsible businesses, entrepreneurs can gain insights into how to create a brand that aligns with their values and makes a positive impact. This may involve adopting eco-friendly practices, supporting causes that align with your brand's values, or creating an employee volunteering program.

Overcoming Fear of Failure When Pursuing Social Impact

One of the biggest challenges entrepreneurs may face when pursuing social impact is a fear of failure. This fear may stem from the belief that social impact initiatives are not directly tied to revenue or profits. However, research has shown that socially responsible companies are more likely to be financially successful in the long run.

To overcome this fear, it is important to shift the focus from short-term gains to long-term impact. By committing to social impact initiatives, entrepreneurs can build a brand that resonates with customers, employees, and stakeholders. Additionally, social impact initiatives can help entrepreneurs attract and retain talent by providing a meaningful work environment.

In conclusion, giving back and making a difference is an essential component of being a successful entrepreneur. By identifying areas where you can make a positive impact, adopting a CSR approach, and creating a sense of purpose, entrepreneurs can build a brand that resonates with their values and makes a positive impact on society.

CHAPTER 20: LEGACY AND LONG-TERM VISION

As entrepreneurs, we often get caught up in the day-to-day operations of our businesses. We focus on short-term goals and forget to think about the long-term impact of our work. However, creating a legacy and having a long-term vision for our businesses is essential for achieving lasting success.

What is legacy, and why is it important?

Legacy can be defined as the impact we make on the world, both in our personal lives and in our businesses. It's what we leave behind for future generations, and it's the way we're remembered by those who come after us.

Legacy is important for several reasons. For one, it gives us a sense of purpose and drives us to do something meaningful with our lives. It also allows us to create something that will outlast us, giving us a sense of immortality.

In business, legacy is important for building a strong brand and a loyal customer base. When we focus on creating something that will be around for years to come, we're more likely to make decisions that will benefit our customers and our employees, rather than just focusing on short-term profits.

Having a long-term vision

A long-term vision for our businesses is key to creating a lasting legacy. A long-term vision allows us to set goals and make decisions that will benefit our businesses in the future, rather than just the present.

To develop a long-term vision, we need to think about where we want our businesses to be in five, ten, or even twenty years. What do we want to accomplish? What impact do we want to make on the world? What kind of company do we want to be remembered as?

Once we have a clear vision of our future, we need to develop a plan for achieving our goals. This might involve expanding our product line, entering new markets, or developing new technologies. We need to be willing to take risks and try new things to achieve our long-term goals.

Importance of succession planning

Succession planning is an essential part of creating a lasting legacy for our businesses. It involves developing a plan for passing on leadership and ownership of our businesses to the next generation of entrepreneurs.

Succession planning is important for several reasons. For one, it ensures that our businesses will continue operating even after we're no longer involved. It also allows us to choose who will take over our businesses, rather than leaving it up to chance.

To develop a succession plan, we need to identify potential successors and provide them with the training and experience they need to take over our businesses. We also need to consider how ownership will be transferred and ensure that we have financial plans in place to fund the transition.

Creating a positive impact

Ultimately, creating a lasting legacy for our businesses is about making a positive impact on the world. We need to consider how our businesses can benefit society, both in the short-term and in the long-term.

This might involve investing in sustainable business practices, giving back to our communities, or developing products and services that improve people's lives.

When we focus on creating a positive impact, we not only benefit society but also ourselves. We feel a sense of fulfillment that goes beyond just making money, and we inspire others to follow in our footsteps.

Learning from successful entrepreneurs

One way to develop a long-term vision and create a lasting legacy is to learn from successful entrepreneurs who have done the same. We can study their businesses, their strategies, and their philosophies to gain insights into how we can build our own legacies.

For example, Steve Jobs had a long-term vision for Apple that extended beyond just creating innovative products. He wanted to change the world and leave a lasting impact. His vision helped Apple become one of the most successful and influential companies of all time.

Similarly, Elon Musk has a long-term vision for his companies that involves making sustainable energy and space exploration accessible to everyone. His businesses, including Tesla and SpaceX, have already made a significant impact on the world and will likely continue to do so for decades to come.

Overcoming fear of the unknown

Developing a long-term vision and creating a lasting legacy can be scary. It requires us to think beyond the present and consider what our businesses will be like in the future. We might be afraid of the unknown and uncertain about whether we can achieve our goals.

However, overcoming this fear is essential for achieving lasting success. We need to be willing to take risks, try new things, and be patient as we work towards our long-term goals.

Living with purpose and intention

Creating a lasting legacy and having a long-term vision for our businesses is about more than just making money. It's about living with purpose and intention and making a positive impact on the world.

As entrepreneurs, we have the power to shape our businesses and our legacies. By developing a long-term vision and focusing on creating a positive impact, we can achieve lasting success and leave a legacy that we can be proud of.

Final Thoughts

As we come to the end of this book, I want to congratulate you on taking the first step towards developing a successful entrepreneur mindset. Remember that this is not a one-time process but rather an ongoing journey of continuous learning and growth.

As you go forward, keep in mind that failure is not the end but rather an opportunity to learn from your mistakes and try again with renewed motivation. Embrace uncertainty as a part of the entrepreneurial journey and use it as fuel to push yourself outside of your comfort zone.

Surround yourself with like-minded individuals who will support and encourage you along the way. Seek out mentors who have been where you are now and can offer guidance based on their own experiences.

Above all, maintain a positive attitude and belief in yourself and your abilities. You have what it takes to become a successful entrepreneur, but it will require hard work, dedication, perseverance, and a willingness to take risks.

I wish you all the best on your journey towards success, and I look forward to hearing about all of your accomplishments. Remember: A successful entrepreneur mindset is within reach if you are willing to put in the effort!

ABOUT THE AUTHOR

Ray Goodwin

Ray Goodwin, is the author behind this series of captivating books on Business Development and self improvement, and has left an indelible mark on the field. He was born and raised in the bustling city of London, where he developed a strong work ethic and an insatiable curiosity about the inner workings of successful businesses. Throughout his illustrious career, Ray leveraged his extensive knowledge and experience to help numerous companies flourish and prosper.

His keen insights and innovative strategies has earned him recognition, driving him to share his expertise with others. Ray believes in the power of sharing knowledge to elevate businesses and empower aspiring entrepreneurs.

Ray's dedication to his craft is evident in the numerous books he has authored on business development and self improvement. His writing style seamlessly blends practical advice, thought-provoking concepts, and real-life case studies, making his books invaluable resources for business professionals and novices alike. His ability to distill complex concepts into accessible language has greatly impacted the lives and careers of countless individuals.

Now retired from the corporate world, Ray and his beloved wife have settled in the idyllic English countryside. Surrounded by the beauty of nature, Ray finds inspiration for his writing and indulges in his hobbies.

Ray Goodwin's books continue to serve as enduring guides for those seeking success in the business world. With a wealth of experience and a deep understanding of the inner workings of businesses, Ray's work remains a testament to his passion for sharing knowledge and helping others flourish.